KNOW YOUR GOVERNMENT

JUDGE

By Jacqueline Laks Gorman
Reading consultant: Susan Nations, M.Ed.,
author/literacy coach/consultant in literacy development

WEEKLY READER®
PUBLISHING

Please visit our web site at www.garethstevens.com
For a free color catalog describing our list of high-quality books,
call 1-800-542-2595 (USA) or 1-800-387-3178 (Canada). Our fax: 1-877-542-2596

Library of Congress Cataloging-in-Publication Data
Laks Gorman, Jacqueline.
    Judge / By Jacqueline Laks Gorman.
        p. cm. — (Know your government)
    Includes bibliographical references and index.
    ISBN-10: 1-4339-0092-0   ISBN-13: 978-1-4339-0092-1 (lib. bdg.)
    ISBN-10: 1-4339-0120-X   ISBN-13: 978-1-4339-0120-1 (softcover)
    1. Judges—United States. I. Title.
KF8775.L35   2008
347.73'14—dc22   2008035518

This edition first published in 2009 by
Weekly Reader® Books
An Imprint of Gareth Stevens Publishing
1 Reader's Digest Road
Pleasantville, NY 10570-7000 USA

Copyright © 2009 by Gareth Stevens, Inc.

Executive Managing Editor: Lisa M. Herrington
Editors: Brian Fitzgerald and Barbara Kiely Miller
Creative Director: Lisa Donovan
Senior Designer: Keith Plechaty
Photo Researchers: Charlene Pinckney and Diane Laska-Swanke
Publisher: Keith Garton

Photo credits: cover & title page © Brooks Kraft/Corbis; p. 5 © Jeff Cadge/Getty Images; p. 6 © David Frazier/
Getty Images; p. 7 Photograph by Steve Petteway, Collection of the Supreme Court of the United States;
p. 9 © David Young-Wolff/Getty Images; p. 10 © Bob Daemmrich/Photo Edit; p. 11 © Jay Freis/Getty Images;
p. 12 United States Department of Agriculture photo by Ken Hammond; p. 13 Photograph by Franz Jantzen,
Collection of the Supreme Court of the United States; p. 15 © Shealah Craighead/The White House;
p. 16 © Ed Clark/Time & Life Pictures/Getty Images; p. 17 © Tim Sloan/AFP/Getty Images; p. 18 Courtesy
Library of Congress; p. 19 Charles Sydney Hopkinson, Collection of the Supreme Court of the United States;
p. 20 © Hank Walker/Time & Life Pictures/Getty Images; p. 21 © Getty Images.

Printed in the United States of America

1 2 3 4 5 6 7 8 9 10 09 08

Cover Photo: In 2006, John Roberts was named chief justice of the U.S. Supreme Court.

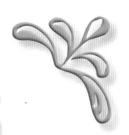

TABLE OF CONTENTS

Words that appear in the glossary are printed in **boldface** type the first time they appear in the text.

CHAPTER 1

Who Are Judges?

Judges are in charge of **courts**. Courts are an important part of our government. The courts interpret, or explain, the law. Courts also decide whether the law has been broken. Judges make sure that people are treated fairly in court.

Lawyers ask people questions during a trial. A judge (center) listens closely to everything that is said.

Trials are held in some courts. During a trial, the court decides whether a person or company broke the law. Law experts, called lawyers, present the facts of the case. The judge makes sure that the trial runs smoothly.

Judges work in different types of courts. Some courts handle crimes. Crimes are acts that break the law. Other courts handle private problems. The problems might be between people or between companies.

A lot happens in a courtroom. A judge is in charge of keeping order.

Judge

Nine justices serve on the Supreme Court. John Roberts (seated, center) is the chief justice.

Each state has its own court system. Cities and towns have courts, too. The Supreme Court is the highest court in the United States. The Supreme Court has one chief judge and eight other judges. These nine men and women are called **justices**.

CHAPTER 2

What Does a Judge Do?

A judge sits in the front of the courtroom. He or she sits behind a desk that is raised above the floor. Judges wear long black robes. Everyone in the courtroom stands when the judge enters the room. The judge makes sure that the trial is fair.

8

Several people help the judge in the courtroom. One person swears in people who will be asked questions. Another person takes notes of everything that is said. People in the courtroom call the judge "Your Honor."

People who will be asked questions in court are sworn in. They raise their right hand and promise to tell the truth.

During a trial, lawyers talk to the jury about the case.

During a trial, the judge also gives directions to the **jury**. The jury is a small group of people in the courtroom. They listen very closely to all the facts. The jury decides whether the **defendant** is innocent or guilty. The defendant is the person or company charged with doing something wrong.

Judges decide which facts can be talked about during a trial. Sometimes experts are called on to give facts.

The jury may decide that the defendant is guilty. Usually the judge then decides the punishment.

Sometimes judges or lawyers make mistakes during trials. Judges who work for an appeals court may review, or go over, the case. If mistakes were made, the judge may order a new trial.

The Supreme Court meets in the Supreme Court building in Washington, D.C.

Congress is part of the **federal** government. Congress makes the laws in the United States. The Supreme Court rules on these laws. The Supreme Court also looks at laws passed by state governments. The Supreme Court decides whether the laws are fair.

The Supreme Court hears about 80 cases every year. The justices meet to talk about each case. Once the Supreme Court rules on a case, the decision is final. All lower courts must follow its decision.

The Supreme Court decides cases in this meeting room. No one is allowed in the room while the Court makes its decision.

CHAPTER 3

How Does a Person Become a Judge?

Judges are usually lawyers. People who want to become lawyers must go to law school after college. Then they must pass special tests. The states have different rules for becoming a state judge.

Samuel Alito was sworn in as a Supreme Court justice in 2006.

The United States has no special rules for becoming a Supreme Court justice. The president picks Supreme Court justices and other important judges. The **Senate** is part of Congress. The Senate must approve the president's choices.

Supreme Court justices serve as long as they want. Some retire when they get old or become sick. Many stay in their jobs until they die. Some justices have served on the Supreme Court for many years.

William O. Douglas served on the Supreme Court for 36 years! That is longer than any other justice.

States have county and city courts, too. Those courts uphold the law in local communities.

In most states, people vote for state judges. In some states, the **governor** or the state **legislature** picks the judges. The legislature is the part of the government that makes laws. Some judges serve for only two years. The top judges in some states can serve as long as they want.

CHAPTER 4

Famous Judges

Many famous judges have served on the Supreme Court. Many people think John Marshall was the greatest justice in history. He became chief justice in 1801. He stayed on the Supreme Court until 1835. He helped make the Court very powerful.

John Marshall

Oliver Wendell Holmes is another famous justice. He joined the Court in 1902. He served until 1932, when he was 90 years old! His ideas were often different from the ideas of other justices. He thought the law should change as the times changed.

Oliver Wendell Holmes was the oldest justice to serve on the Supreme Court.

Thurgood Marshall was an important lawyer. He fought for **civil rights**. He became a Supreme Court justice in 1967. He was the first African American justice. He retired in 1991. In the same year, Clarence Thomas became the second African American justice.

In 1967, Thurgood Marshall became the first African American on the Supreme Court.

Sandra Day O'Connor was the first woman to serve on the Supreme Court. She served from 1981 until 2006. In 1993, Ruth Bader Ginsburg became the second woman on the Supreme Court.

Like all judges, they worked to make sure that people are treated fairly under the law.

Sandra Day O'Connor was the first woman on the Supreme Court.

Glossary

civil rights: the rights of personal freedom guaranteed to every person in a country

courts: the places where legal cases are heard and decided

defendant: in a court case, the person or company that is charged with doing something wrong

federal: national. The federal government is the government of the whole United States.

governor: the head of a state government

jury: a small group of people who decide during a trial whether someone has broken the law

justices: the judges who sit on the U.S. Supreme Court

legislature: the part of the government that makes the laws

Senate: one of the two parts of Congress. The other part is the House of Representatives.

trials: the official processes of deciding in a court of law whether someone did something wrong

To Find Out More

Books

Law and Order. Citizens and Their Governments (series).
Kathleen G. Manatt (Cherry Lake, 2007)

Sandra Day O'Connor. Remarkable People (series).
Jennifer Howse (Weigl Publishers, 2007)

What's the Supreme Court? First Guide to Government (series).
Nancy Harris (Heinemann, 2007)

Web Sites

Inside the Courtroom
www.usdoj.gov/usao/eousa/kidspage
Learn what happens in a federal courtroom.

King County Superior Court Kids Web Site
www.metrokc.gov/kcsc/kids/kids_index.htm
Learn how the courts work and how people who break the law get
sent to jail!

Index

About the Author

Jacqueline Laks Gorman is a writer and an editor. She grew up in New York City. She has worked on many kinds of books and has written several children's series. She lives with her husband, David, and children, Colin and Caitlin, in DeKalb, Illinois. She registered to vote when she turned 18 and votes in every election.